This book **belongs to**

SOLE SURVIVOR

SURVIVING THE ICE

Louise Spilsbury

Gareth Stevens
PUBLISHING

Please visit our website, www.garethstevens.com.
For a free color catalog of all our high-quality books,
call toll free 1-800-542-2595 or fax 1-877-542-2596.

CATALOGING-IN-PUBLICATION DATA

Names: Spilsbury, Louise.
Title: Surviving the ice / Louise Spilsbury.
Description: New York : Gareth Stevens Publishing, 2017. | Series: Sole survivor |
    Includes index.
Identifiers: ISBN 9781482450873 (pbk.) | ISBN 9781482450897 (library bound) |
    ISBN 9781482450880 (6 pack)
Subjects: LCSH: Survival--Polar regions--Juvenile literature. | Polar regions--
    Environmental conditions--Juvenile literature.
Classification: LCC GF86.S65 2017| DDC 363.34092'211--dc23

Published in 2017 by
Gareth Stevens Publishing
111 East 14th Street, Suite 349
New York, NY 10003

Copyright © 2017 Gareth Stevens Publishing

Produced for Gareth Stevens by Calcium
Editors: Sarah Eason and Jennifer Sanderson
Designer: Paul Myerscough

Picture credits: Cover: Shutterstock: Furtseff (right), Warren Goldswain (left).
Inside: Dreamstime: Jonathan Lingel 13, David Máška 12–13; Shutterstock:
Marcos Amend 32–33, Denis Burdin 38–39, Brenda Carson 18–19, Przemyslaw
Ceynowa 8–9, Critterbiz 28–29, Piotr Debowski 24–25, Ericlefrancais 28, Footage
Pro 34–35, Colman Lerner Gerardo 38, Halfpoint 9, HektoR 1, 40–41, HomeArt
22, Incredible Arctic 40, Marcel Jancovic 27, Yongyut Kumsri 42, Vitezslav
Malina 36–37, Jan Mika 37, Dudarev Mikhail 6–7, MP CZ 10–11, Tyler Olson 26–27,
Jens Ottoson 5, 16–17, 22–23, Photodynamic 4–5, Severe 21, Smit 14–15, Joseph
Sohm 42–43, Vitalliy 35, Christopher Wood 30–31, ZinaidaSopina 20–21.

Printed in the United States of America
CPSIA compliance information: Batch #CS16GS
For further information contact Gareth Stevens, New York, New York at 1-800-542-2595.

CONTENTS

Chapter One

ICE DANGERS

The Arctic and the Antarctic are covered in ice and they are the coldest places on our planet. The Arctic is the region of the world around the North Pole. It is a huge, frozen ocean. In winter, temperatures there can drop below -67 degrees Fahrenheit (-55 °C).

The Antarctic is at the South Pole and includes the **continent** of Antarctica and the ocean around it. There, temperatures can drop to below -100 degrees Fahrenheit (-73 °C) in winter. These icy worlds are incredibly beautiful to look at, but visitors should beware: the harsh weather conditions can be deadly.

Some people visit the South Pole for the spectacular views and to see the cute penguins that live on the ice.

At the North Pole, amazing, colorful displays of natural light can be seen in the night sky.

How to Survive

Icy winds can freeze exposed skin in seconds and blizzards (snowstorms) can reduce visibility to a few feet. It is easy to get lost in endless expanses of snow and ice. To survive, there are some basic rules everyone should follow:

- Plan trips carefully.
- Always carry a survival bag containing a tent, water, food, and a stove.
- Wear suitable clothing for protection against the fast winds and the cold and damp.
- Carry a **global positioning system (GPS)** device, a **satellite phone**, and a beacon that helps rescuers find lost people.
- Visit the area as part of a group as there is safety in numbers.

In this book, we are going to look at some of the hazards people face in the Arctic and Antarctic, and how some people have survived the most terrifying disasters of all.

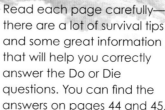
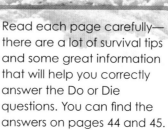

Read each page carefully— there are a lot of survival tips and some great information that will help you correctly answer the Do or Die questions. You can find the answers on pages 44 and 45.

KEEPING WARM

One of the biggest dangers facing travelers to the Arctic and Antarctic is freezing. At the Arctic, it is very cold and there is the added danger of falling into the icy ocean. At the Antarctic, the cold is made worse by high winds that blow warmth away from the body. They also blow into clothing, replacing warm air with cold air. Getting very cold can cause a life-threatening condition called **hypothermia**.

The normal human body temperature is 98.6 degrees Fahrenheit (37 °C). Hypothermia occurs when a person's body temperature drops below 95 degrees Fahrenheit (35 °C). At this temperature, the body cannot function properly, so it starts to shut down. People begin to mumble, stumble around, and get confused and sleepy. If hypothermia is not treated immediately, people can die. It is vital that sufferers warm up again quickly.

"I SURVIVED..."

TOM CREAN IS A LEGENDARY ANTARCTIC EXPLORER. ON A TRIP TO THE SOUTH POLE IN 1912, HE HAD TO WALK ON HIS OWN FOR 35 MILES (56.3 KM) TO REACH A RESCUE TEAM. HE WAS HOPING TO SAVE TWO SICK COLLEAGUES. CREAN HAD NO PROPER SURVIVAL CLOTHING, JUST LAYERS OF SWEATERS THAT FROZE WITH HIS SWEAT, AND JUST A FEW COOKIES TO EAT. NO ONE REALLY KNOWS HOW HE SURVIVED THE TRIP WITHOUT SUFFERING HYPOTHERMIA.

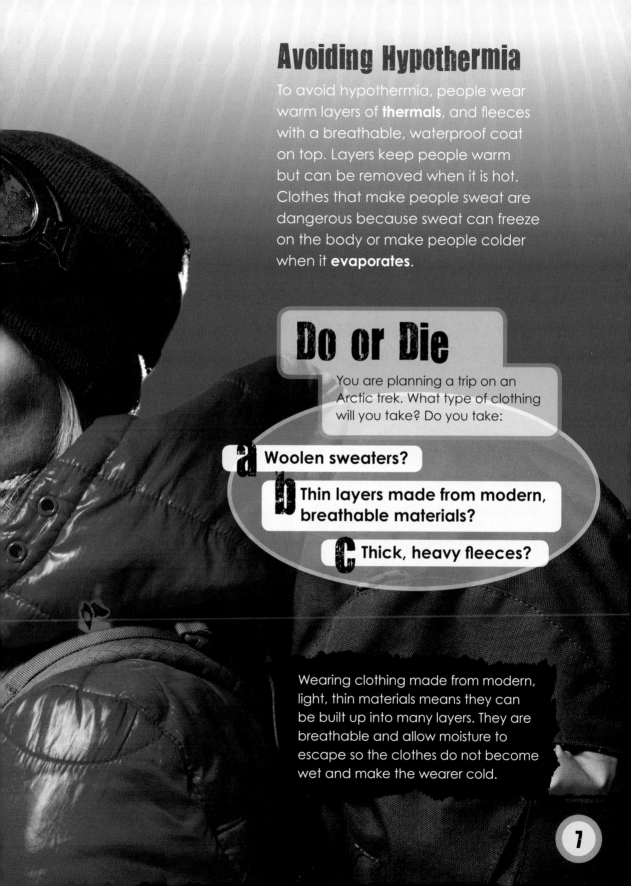

Avoiding Hypothermia

To avoid hypothermia, people wear warm layers of **thermals**, and fleeces with a breathable, waterproof coat on top. Layers keep people warm but can be removed when it is hot. Clothes that make people sweat are dangerous because sweat can freeze on the body or make people colder when it **evaporates**.

Do or Die

You are planning a trip on an Arctic trek. What type of clothing will you take? Do you take:

a Woolen sweaters?

b Thin layers made from modern, breathable materials?

c Thick, heavy fleeces?

Wearing clothing made from modern, light, thin materials means they can be built up into many layers. They are breathable and allow moisture to escape so the clothes do not become wet and make the wearer cold.

FROSTBITE

Frostbite is a painful condition that occurs when parts of the body are exposed to severe cold. It happens because when people get very cold, their body diverts blood flow from the extremities—parts such as the fingers, nose, and toes—to keep the most important body parts warm. When blood flow leaves the extremities for too long, the **tissues** there die.

In the early stages of frostbite, affected parts look red and feel cold and sore. If the parts are warmed up, new tissue will replace the old tissue and the part will heal. If frostbite is left, the parts will turn pale, sting, burn, and swell. If this is not treated quickly, the parts become black and hard, and may have to be **amputated**.

Avoiding Frostbite

Frostbite usually affects the hands, feet, ears, nose, cheeks, chin, and lips. To avoid it, people should keep these extremities well covered. They should wear gloves, wrap scarves over their chin, nose and mouth, and pull a warm hood over their ears and forehead. It is also important to keep feet warm and dry.

A good-quality pair of gloves should keep hands warm and dry even when handling snow and ice.

Toe Trouble

An explorer's feet can be at the highest risk from frostbite, because they are in constant contact with the icy ground. It is important to wear boots that fit correctly, and that have an **insulating** layer and an outer shell. Most explorers also wear a thin pair of socks under a thicker pair. Many people also wear an oversock, which is a waterproof barrier that covers their whole boot.

As soon as hands feel very cold, people should warm up their fingers to prevent frostbite.

Do or Die

You are planning a long trek in the Antarctic and you need a new pair of boots. Do you:

a Go to a specialist and make sure you get a pair that fits perfectly?

b Order a pair of boots online?

c Wear a pair of walking boots you already own?

NEVER-ENDING SUN

The polar regions are called the "lands of the midnight sun." This is because in the summer, the sun never sets. Earth is tilted at an angle and it **orbits** the sun, which means the North Pole is always pointing toward the sun in summer and gets continuous sunlight. It points away from the sun in winter, making it dark all day and night. The poles have opposite seasons, so while the North Pole is in constant darkness, the South Pole is in constant sunlight and vice versa.

When the sun shines all day every day, this puts explorers at risk of sunburn. They may feel chilled to the bone, but their skin is exposed to harsh **ultraviolet (UV)** rays. The risk of sunburn is even greater because of all the snow and ice at the poles. Sunlight reflects off the white surface of snow and ice and hits the skin again.

Surviving Sunburn

To avoid sunburn, explorers need to keep skin covered and wear strong sunblock on any exposed body parts, such as the lips, chin, ears, and even under the nose. Even on overcast days, they should also wear sunglasses or snow goggles with side shields to reduce the risk of getting **snow blindness**.

Inuit Snow Goggles

People who have lost their sunglasses can improvise and make snow goggles like those used by Inuit people. The Inuit wore bands of leather over their eyes, with narrow slits cut into the material. The slits allow people to see, while reducing the amount of sunlight that hits their eyes.

Polar explorers must wear sunglasses or goggles even on a cloudy day, because when the sun's rays reflect off the snow, they can burn eyes.

Do or Die

You are on an expedition in the Arctic when you lose your sunglasses. Do you:

a Make a pair of sunglasses using a piece of fabric with slits cut into it?

b Keep going regardless because it is a cloudy day?

c Walk with your hand shielding your eyes?

Chapter Two

SHELTER

Even if explorers are wearing the correct clothing, they need to cope with icy temperatures at the poles. They must get inside a shelter at bedtime or face the real risk of freezing to death. When people stop walking and moving around, they can become cold very quickly. It is vital they go into a shelter that keeps out the winds and ice, and hides them from any **predators.**

Scientists who stay at the polar regions for long periods of time, to study the environment there, live in purpose-built shelters. They live in huts built from parts that they bring with them. They also have electricity **generators** that power heaters that keep people warm. Some huts are on stilts to keep them off the cold, icy ground.

Pitching a Tent

Some ice explorers use tents. Dome-shaped tents are good for withstanding high winds and windblown snow and ice. Stakes cannot be pushed firmly into snow and ice, so when pitching a tent, people tie guy ropes to rocks and put rocks inside the tent. This keeps the strong winds from lifting the tent off the ground and blowing it away.

Time for Bed

You may have noticed how cold it gets when you sit on cold ground. When explorers go to bed in a tent, they often sleep in a special sleeping bag fitted with an inflatable thermal mattress. This keeps people off the ice and helps them keep warm. They cover themselves with insulated sleeping bags or sheepskins.

This is the entrance to a South Pole research station once used to protect researchers from the elements.

These tents will protect explorers from the heavy snowfall that has forced them to stop for a few days.

Do or Die

You are an Antarctic explorer working far from your base. When it is time to sleep, do you:

a Put up a tent tied to rocks, and use rocks to weigh it down?

b Put on an extra coat and lie behind a rock?

c Put up a tent and put the tent pegs into the ice?

SNOW SHELTERS

If people become stranded at the Poles without a shelter, they will need to build a snow shelter. Snow is mostly air, which makes it a good insulating material. People can make several different kinds of snow shelter. Most importantly, the shelter should not be too big—it should be large enough only for the person to lie down inside it, with space to build a fire, too, if people can find enough wood to burn.

People can build snow shelters in the form of an igloo if they can find snow set hard enough to cut into blocks. They need a saw to cut thick, rectangular blocks. The best way to build an igloo is with a circular base. As people build up the sides of the igloo, they should position the blocks so they lean inward. The blocks at the top of the igloo will then meet to form a **dome**-shaped roof.

"I SURVIVED..."

IN 1934, RICHARD E. BYRD BECAME THE FIRST MAN TO SPEND A WINTER ALONE IN ANTARCTICA WHEN HE WAS MANNING A WEATHER STATION. HE COULD NOT LEAVE HIS HUT BECAUSE OF THE HURRICANE-FORCE WINDS OUTSIDE. INSIDE, HIS STOVE WAS RELEASING DEADLY **CARBON MONOXIDE** FUMES. HE HAD TO USE IT AS LITTLE AS POSSIBLE AND SPEND HOURS SITTING IN DARKNESS UNTIL SPRING CAME AND HE COULD GO OUTSIDE AGAIN.

Snow Tunnel

People can also make a shelter by digging a tunnel into a bank of snow. At the end of the tunnel, they can carve out a space in which to sleep. The walls of any shelter should be at least 1 foot (30 cm) thick, to keep out the wind and cold.

The entrance to an igloo should be small and low, to keep cold winds from getting in. Once inside, people block the entrance for the same reason.

Do or Die

Your tent blows away in the wind and you have to build a shelter in the snow. You have a shovel but not a saw. Do you build:

a An igloo?

b A tunnel with narrow walls?

c A tunnel cave with thick walls?

Chapter Three

FOOD AND WATER

Food and water are always necessary for survival, but in icy conditions, the body needs them more than ever. This is because when it is cold, the body uses extra **calories** to create more heat as it tries to keep itself warm. It also takes more energy to do things in a harsh polar environment. Even simple activities, like walking and working, require more calories than usual.

The recommended intake for an adult man is 2,500 calories a day, but the daily target for a polar explorer is at least 5,000–7,000 calories. If the explorer is very active, they may need even more calories to stay healthy.

Hidden Calories

When explorers plan a trip to the polar regions, a large supply of high-calorie food is one of the most important things on their list. When on a daily expedition away from a base, it is also vital they take some of these foodstuffs with their other emergency supplies. Some tricks people use to increase their intake of calories is to melt butter into their evening meal or to eat high-calorie snacks, such as macadamia nuts.

Water Works

It is easy for people to become **dehydrated** at the poles because the air is so dry there. Dehydration is dangerous because if it occurs, the body cannot regulate its temperature and becomes tired and stressed.

Do or Die

You are planning a trip away from base camp for a day and do not have a lot of space in your backpack. Do you take:

a Just a snack because you do not feel hungry?

b High-calorie food for the day and extra for emergencies?

c A light meal and snacks for one day?

Along with taking food for the length of time people plan to be on a trip, they should also take extra supplies in case they are stranded at any point.

CATCHING FOOD

When people get lost without food supplies in the Arctic or Antarctic, they face a real challenge. It is too cold in these regions for many plants to grow. With few plants to eat, few animals can live in the **habitat**. Some animals, such as Arctic hares and small rodents, live in polar regions in the summer months. They can be trapped for food. People can also catch fish and other animals in or near the water.

Many fish have **adapted** to live in icy waters, and seabirds, seals, and other animals feed on them. Some people have survived by eating these animals, and in the Antarctic, they have eaten penguins. To keep warm in polar conditions, seals and penguins have thick layers of fat, called **blubber**, which can provide people with a lot of calories.

"I SURVIVED..."

IN 1923, A WOMAN NAMED ADA BLACKJACK AND FOUR MEN SET OUT ON AN EXPEDITION TO A BLEAK ARCTIC ISLAND. AFTER BECOMING TRAPPED BY ICE, THREE OF THE MEN LEFT ADA LOOKING AFTER THE INJURED FOURTH MAN TO WALK ACROSS THE FROZEN OCEAN FOR HELP. THEY WERE NEVER SEEN AGAIN. AFTER THE FOURTH MAN DIED, TO SURVIVE, ADA TRAPPED FOXES AND HUNTED SEALS FOR FOOD. SHE SURVIVED AND MADE IT BACK TO HER SON IN ALASKA.

Catching Fish

In the Arctic, people sometimes catch fish by breaking a hole about 8 inches (20 cm) wide through the ice, and catching the fish in a net or on a fishing line. Care must be taken with this method in case the ice cracks toward where people are standing. Another option is to collect shellfish, such as mussels, from the edge of ice. However, some, such as the Arctic mussel, are poisonous.

This man has set up a device to catch fish from beneath the ice on a frozen lake.

Do or Die

You are stranded on Arctic ice and you have run out of food. To catch fish, do you:

a Carefully make a small hole in the ice and catch fish in a net?

b Smash a very large hole in the ice and catch fish in a net?

c Make a hole and catch fish with your bare hands?

GETTING WATER

Air at the poles is so dry that the human body loses water just by breathing. People need to drink at least 1.6 to 2.1 gallons (6 to 8 L) of water a day. In theory, this should be easy because water is found everywhere at the poles. However, it is in the form of snow and ice. Melting snow in the mouth to drink the water is not an option. If people do this, it makes their body colder and increases the risk of hypothermia.

In the summer months, people might be able to get water from streams, springs, creeks, and lakes at the edges of the polar regions. Even in places closer to the poles, there may be pools of melted ice. Before drinking this water, it should be **filtered**, to purify it. Otherwise, people risk drinking **contaminated** or dirty water that could make them sick.

At the poles, people are surrounded by ice and snow, but they should not melt either in their mouth to make water.

Melting Water

In the winter months or when melted water is hard to come by, people melt snow and ice to make their own drinking water. They collect snow and ice and melt it slowly in a pan over a stove. It is possible to get more water from ice than the same volume of snow.

Arctic Ice

It is important to remember that the Arctic is a frozen ocean and so Arctic ice is formed from seawater. Seawater contains salt, which makes it dangerous for people to drink. However, over time, the salt drains out of ice and it becomes safe to melt and drink. To identify ice that is safe to melt and drink, people look at the color of the ice. New seawater ice is gray-white, but old sea ice is blue in color and easily breaks.

It does not take long to build a fire and melt snow to make water that is safe to drink.

Do or Die

You run out of water on a trip in the Arctic and need to use ice to get water to drink. Do you:

a Melt ice in your mouth?

b Melt gray-white ice over a stove?

c Melt blue ice that breaks easily?

Chapter Four

ON THE MOVE

Usually, when people travel, there are landmarks or features that help them find their way. However, this is not the case when moving around an icy landscape. The barren, icy landscape of the poles is difficult to **navigate** because everything looks the same. There are few landmarks because much of the surface is flat, white, and featureless. Without the right equipment, people can easily get lost, and travel around in circles.

The weather can change quickly at the poles. High winds can suddenly bring snow clouds that make the landscape look different. Gusts of wind can also blow and move snow, so views quickly change. Clouds and sea mist can fill the air and make it difficult to see far ahead.

It is easy for people to lose their way in a landscape covered in ice and snow.

Walking on Thin Ice

The other difficulty when traveling on ice at the Arctic is that some areas of ice are thinner than others, and people can fall through it. The color of ice can help people figure out if it is safe to walk onward, or if they should retrace their steps.

Black Ice

Black ice is dangerous. It is freshly made, and if people step on it, they are likely to fall through. Gray ice is slightly older and a little thicker. It might support someone on skis, because their weight is distributed over a wider area. However, walkers may fall through. The safest ice is white ice, which is usually at least 6 to 12 inches (15 to 30 cm) thick.

The color of ice can be an indication of how safe it is to walk on.

Do or Die

You are trekking across ice with a group and you are leading at the front. You have to decide which path of ice is the safest. Do you choose:

 **a** Gray ice?

 **b** Black ice?

 **c** White ice?

FINDING THE WAY

No explorers set off on polar ice without navigation equipment. The most basic tool is a compass. A compass contains a magnetized needle that always points north because it lines up with Earth's lines of magnetic force. To the left of north is west. To the right of north is east. Directly below north is south. A compass is particularly useful because it does not require batteries to work. Batteries can die or freeze.

Most explorers at the poles use a device with a GPS. They use the device to figure out where they are, and create maps that help them find the direction in which they need to travel.

"I SURVIVED..."

In 2012, solo skier Felicity Aston skied more than 1,000 miles (1,609 km) across Antarctica. Much of the snowy terrain of Antarctica is flat, so there are few landmarks to help guide the way. It is also light at night in the Antarctic summer, so Felicity could not navigate using the stars. Another problem the skier had was that her compass was unreliable so close to the magnetic South Pole, so she instead relied on GPS.

Old-Fashioned Methods

If people lose their navigation equipment, they can still survive if they know what to look for. People can navigate using the position of the sun in the sky, and the stars at night. Seabirds can help, too, because they usually fly back toward land at the end of the day.

Do or Die

You are lost on polar ice but you have a compass and you know you need to head west. Do you:

a Go to the left of the direction the compass points?

b Go in the opposite direction the compass points?

c Go to the right of the direction the compass points?

The first person to reach the North Pole did so using a compass. A compass is still a useful navigation tool.

GETTING AROUND

People arrive at polar regions by airplane or on giant ships called **icebreakers**. Icebreakers have very strong **hulls** that can carve a path through sheets of ice floating on the water's surface. Planes that travel to icy landscapes have large skis that they can lower to land on ice or snow.

To travel long distances across ice and snow, people use snowmobiles. Snowmobiles are motorized sleds. They have rubber tracks with rough treads to keep them from sinking and help them grip slippery snow. Snowmobiles have engines that run on fuel and can travel at up to 80 miles per hour (50 kph) across flat snow and ice. In some places, people still use sleds pulled by packs of dogs.

Special Vehicles

Some teams also use tractors or Sno-cats® with **caterpillar tracks** that can tow large sleds carrying supplies. Hägglund trucks are large vehicles with very wide tracks that can cross bumpy surfaces, and they can float if they break through ice into Arctic water. Some vehicles are fitted with a snowplow that can clear snow if it piles up and blocks buildings where vehicles are stored or people are staying.

Most snowmobiles are designed for one or two people and have skis at the front that are used to steer the vehicle.

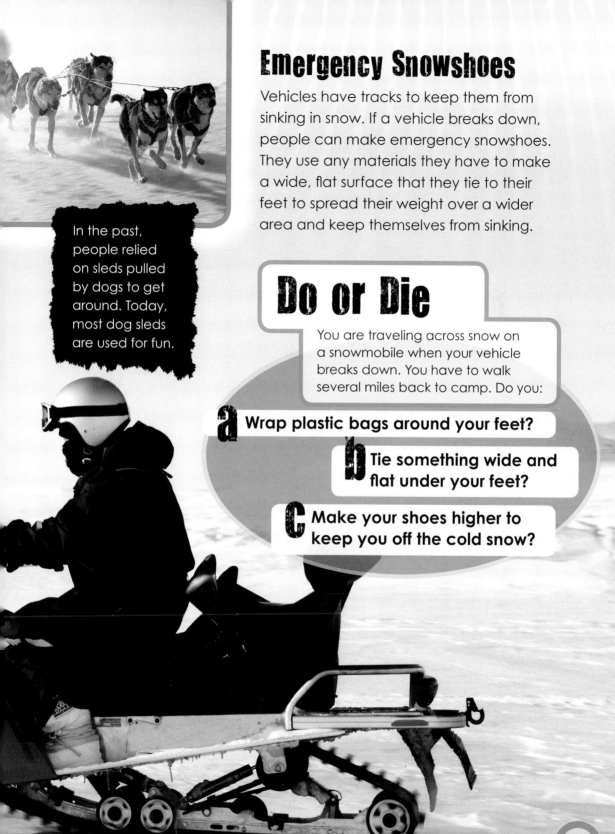

Emergency Snowshoes

Vehicles have tracks to keep them from sinking in snow. If a vehicle breaks down, people can make emergency snowshoes. They use any materials they have to make a wide, flat surface that they tie to their feet to spread their weight over a wider area and keep themselves from sinking.

In the past, people relied on sleds pulled by dogs to get around. Today, most dog sleds are used for fun.

Do or Die

You are traveling across snow on a snowmobile when your vehicle breaks down. You have to walk several miles back to camp. Do you:

a Wrap plastic bags around your feet?

b Tie something wide and flat under your feet?

c Make your shoes higher to keep you off the cold snow?

Chapter Five

UNDER ATTACK!

Life is tough for animals at the poles. Only those with special adaptations to help them cope with the cold, the winds, and the lack of water can survive there. Some animals, such as the rock ptarmigan bird, survive by making a burrow under the snow. Antarctic cod make a substance in their blood that acts like **antifreeze**, which keeps their bodies from freezing.

One reason large animals, such as polar bears and leopard seals, survive at the poles is their size. Big animals have a smaller surface area-to-volume ratio than small animals, which helps them reduce heat loss. They are also powerful and deadly predators that can catch food. This makes them very dangerous to humans visiting the poles.

Human Prey

Very few people visit the poles, so animal attacks are rare. Most animals do not seek human **prey**, but they may attack if they are frightened or provoked, if they are starving, or if they think they need to attack to protect their young.

When a wolf opens its mouth and bites, its jaws are strong enough to crush big bones.

Arctic Wolves

Arctic wolves live in packs and work together to bring down weak or old members of a musk ox or caribou herd. They also eat Arctic hares and lemmings. If people meet a wolf in the wild, they should back away slowly if they can. If a wolf acts aggressively, they should look it in the eyes, shout loudly, yell, and clap. This should make it run away. People should not turn their back on wolves or run away.

One reason wolves howl is to call to the other wolves in the pack to hunt.

Do or Die

You are outside the safety of your camp when you encounter an aggressive Arctic wolf. Should you:

a Turn around and run?

b Act as if you are unafraid, shout, and yell?

c Avoid eye contact and stay quiet?

POLAR BEARS

Polar bears are beautiful animals that look adorable on a Christmas card, but they can be deadly in real life. The polar bear is the world's largest land carnivore. Polar bears do not normally attack humans, but if a bear is very hungry, it might try to catch and kill a human, so it can feed itself and its cubs. The bears may also attack if they are frightened.

Polar bears usually hunt seals, although they may also eat small land mammals and berries. Their white fur **camouflages** them against the snow, so they can sneak up on prey. When they get close to prey, they can then run or swim quickly for a short time to catch it. They also catch seals that come up to breathe through holes in the ice.

Polar Bear Power

Polar bears are dangerous because they are very strong and grow to more than 8 feet (2.5 m) long. They have powerful legs, sharp teeth, and massive claws. They can knock out people or even kill them with one swipe from their paws. Polar bears can run faster than a human so people cannot outrun them.

Escaping Polar Bears

The best way to avoid polar bear attacks is to stay away from the bears. People should avoid attracting bears by storing food in airtight containers. Explorers should also carry **pepper spray** to spray at bears. The spray makes the bear's eyes sting, giving people time to run away. People should also carry flares or firecrackers that can scare away bears. Explorers should always travel in a group of two or more people, and stay together if a bear approaches.

> Polar bears are the world's largest land-living predators.

Do or Die

You are on a polar expedition when a bear approaches. What should you do to avoid getting hurt? Do you:

a Walk toward the bear?

b Spray pepper spray at it?

c Lie down?

LEOPARD SEALS

Leopard seals are found on the ice around the edges of the Antarctic continent. They are named for their black-spotted coat, which is similar to that of a leopard. Like leopards, these creatures are also fierce predators. They feed on smaller seals, fish, and squid, and, sometimes, come up beneath seabirds resting on the water's surface. Like most other seals, leopard seals are insulated from icy Antarctic waters by a thick layer of blubber.

Leopard seals have large front flippers that they use to move and steer through the water. They can swim so fast that they can jump out of the water to attack prey on the edge of the ice. When hunting, they also lurk underwater near an ice shelf, and snatch animals just as they enter the water after jumping off the ice.

Avoiding Attack

Leopard seals have a huge mouth, powerful jaws, and long teeth. They pose a threat to humans, too. Some attacks may happen because seals mistake humans for seals. To be safe, people should keep away from the edge of **ice sheets** and avoid getting in water if a leopard seal is there.

The leopard seal's teeth are razor sharp and they are the only seal capable of attacking a human.

Do or Die

You are walking in the Antarctic where there is a threat of leopard seals. What is the most important advice you should follow? Should you:

a Go in a group?

b Keep alert at all times?

c Keep away from the edge of the ice?

"I SURVIVED..."

IN 2011, EXPERIENCED ANTARCTIC PHOTOGRAPHER PAUL NICKLEN WAS UNDERWATER SNAPPING THE BIGGEST LEOPARD SEAL HE HAD EVER SEEN. IT SUDDENLY DROPPED THE PENGUIN IT HAD CAUGHT, SWAM AT PAUL, AND OPENED ITS JAWS, ENGULFING PAUL'S CAMERA AND HEAD! PAUL WAS TERRIFIED BUT KEPT STILL, SO THE SEAL KNEW HE WAS NOT A THREAT. IT WENT AWAY, CAUGHT A FRESH PENGUIN, AND BROUGHT IT TO PAUL AS A FOOD GIFT!

Chapter Six

NATURAL HAZARDS

The remote Arctic and Antarctic regions are full of natural hazards caused by the extremes of weather. Strong winds can blow constantly at more than 100 miles per hour (160 kph), and can blow snow into great clouds that make it impossible for people to see a hand in front of their face. The weather also changes fast. What may begin as a clear, sunny day can become dangerous in minutes.

Only researchers live in Antarctica and few people live in the Arctic regions because the **climate** is too harsh. Even getting to these places can be treacherous. Most people travel by ship through waters that are rocked by high, rough waves, and scattered with sheets of sea ice that are constantly shifting and changing.

If the sea freezes, it can trap most ships, but icebreaker ships, like this one, are made to break through ice.

If someone steps on thin ice and it breaks, they could find themselves freezing in deep, icy water.

Sea Ice

Sea ice is frozen ocean water. It forms, grows, and melts with the changing seasons. **Climate change** is increasing the amount of ice that melts every year. This makes it dangerous for scientists who work on sea ice because of the danger of falling through thin ice, or being on a piece of ice that breaks off and floats away. That is why they carry poles to check the thickness of ice they walk on.

Pack Ice

In winter, as water freezes into ice again, large sheets of floating sea ice, called pack ice, form. These can be several feet thick and they can change in a matter of hours from being open to packed tight. They can trap or even crush ships.

Do or Die

You are helping scientists study the effects of climate change on sea ice. What do you use to check the thickness of the ice you walk on?

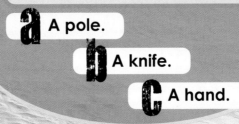

a A pole.

b A knife.

c A hand.

BLIZZARDS

Blizzards are powerful, dangerous snowstorms. In a blizzard, fast swirling winds blow large amounts of snow around in the air at high speeds. Blizzards are often called whiteouts because the swirling snow in the air makes everything look white, and it becomes impossible to see where you are or where you are going. People often cannot hear because of the loud, roaring sound the wind makes.

In a blizzard, people can get lost in a matter of seconds, and may freeze to death before being found. That is why people hang "blizz lines" between the buildings that form polar camps. Blizz lines are ropes that people can hold onto to keep them from being blown away. They can also follow the ropes to guide them to safety if they cannot see.

It is impossible to see where one is going in a blizzard or whiteout.

"I SURVIVED..."

WHEN KEIZO FUNATSU WENT OUTSIDE HIS TENT DURING AN ANTARCTIC EXPEDITION, TO FEED SLED DOGS, THE BLIZZARD WAS NOT BAD. SUDDENLY, IT WORSENED AND HE WAS LOST. HE USED A PAIR OF PLIERS TO DIG A DITCH IN THE ICE, AND CURLED UP IN IT. EVERY HALF HOUR, HE GOT OUT AND JUMPED AROUND TO KEEP WARM. AFTER A TERRIBLE NIGHT AND WITH FROSTBITE AFFECTING HIS FEET, HE FINALLY HEARD RESCUERS CALLING HIS NAME AND WAS SAVED.

In a blizzard, the eyes, nose, and mouth can be covered by or filled with snow very quickly.

Do or Die

You are working outside at a research camp in the Antarctic when a blizzard hits. Do you:

a Run in the direction you think a hut is?

b Grab the nearest blizz line?

c Shout for help?

Training for Blizzards

Before going on an expedition, people train for blizzards. For example, they wear white buckets on their heads so they cannot see. This helps them learn to depend upon other people. They are also taught to hold onto a rope as they search an area for a missing person.

ICEBERGS

Icebergs look like huge, ice mountains that float in the sea, however, they are not sea ice. An iceberg is a large piece of freshwater ice that has broken off the end of a **glacier** that juts over the sea. A glacier is a frozen river of ice that flows over land in Antarctica and the Arctic. Glaciers move very slowly toward the sea. Icebergs drift away from land, into open water.

Sometimes, icebergs flip over suddenly, creating giant waves, called tsunamis, that smash into everything in their paths. Icebergs are also dangerous because they are sharp and rock-hard. If a ship hits them, they make a hole in its hull that can sink a vessel very quickly. The most famous ship sunk by an iceberg was the *Titanic*. It sunk in 1912.

When part of a glacier breaks off, it becomes an iceberg that floats in the sea.

Hidden Danger

Icebergs can be as small as a car or as big as a small country. The feature that makes all icebergs dangerous is that 99 percent of their bulk is hidden under the water. Only the tip of an iceberg is visible. Because the largest part is under the water, it can damage a boat that, at the water's surface, seems far away from the iceberg.

International Ice Patrol

After the *Titanic* sank and killed more than 1,500 people, an International Ice Patrol (IIP) was set up. This organization uses aircraft to spot icebergs and collects ships' reports about icebergs. It loads this information onto the Internet so other ships can check where icebergs are, and plan routes that avoid these hidden dangers.

Ships use **radar** to spot icebergs, but there are still iceberg strikes on boats every year.

Do or Die

You are on a ship navigating its way through the icy waters of the Arctic. To make sure you do not hit an iceberg, do you:

a Order the crew to look out for icebergs?

b Check IIP reports about iceberg sightings?

c Travel in a ship with a reinforced hull?

DEEP CREVASSES

A crevasse is a deep crack in a glacier or ice sheet. They usually form in the top 160 feet (50 m) of a glacier, where the ice is brittle. Crevasses also form as the ice constantly shifts, because different parts of a glacier move at varying speeds down a slope. Crevasses can be deadly. If people fall into them, they can fall 100 feet (30 m) or more to their deaths.

Some glaciers are riddled with visible crevasses, like this one in the Arctic.

What makes crevasses especially dangerous is that they can be hidden. A frozen bridge of snow can form over a crevasse, and hide it from people walking over its surface. A snow bridge is thin, so it cracks easily when people walk over it. People can find themselves tumbling headlong into a frozen ravine, or even into an ocean.

In this photograph you can see how deep and wide a crevasse can be below its narrow opening at the top.

40

Crevasse Care

When walking in areas where crevasses are common, groups of two or three people tie themselves together with ropes about 150 feet (45 m) long. That way, if one person falls, the others can keep them from falling too far, and then pull them out. If one person falls into a crevasse, they should stretch out their body to avoid falling farther.

"I SURVIVED..."

IN 1911, DOUGLAS MAWSON WAS ON AN ANTARCTIC EXPEDITION. HIS TEAMMATES HAD DIED AND HE HAD LOST ALL HIS EQUIPMENT. ALONE AND WEAK, HE WAS WALKING ACROSS THE ICE WHEN, SUDDENLY, HE FELL THROUGH A SNOW BRIDGE INTO A HIDDEN CREVASSE. LUCKILY, THE SLED TO WHICH HE WAS TIED BECAME STUCK IN THE SNOW ABOVE. MAWSON PULLED HIMSELF UP, USING A ROPE, AND MANAGED TO CLIMB OUT OF THE HOLE TO SAFETY.

Do or Die

You are walking with friends in the Antarctic in a group of 12. How many separate ropes will you need to tie yourselves together for safety?

a One.

b Two.

c Four.

BE PREPARED

The Arctic and Antarctic are stunningly beautiful wildernesses, and every year, more people visit them for study, work, or leisure. If people are well-prepared, have the correct equipment, and know what to do in an emergency, they can safely visit polar regions. However, there are always risks because the weather can quickly change there, and conditions are extreme.

To be prepared, people must buy the right gear. To survive at the poles, people need to be able to stay dry and warm. They need layers of lightweight, breathable and warm clothes, and a windproof and waterproof jacket. In barren, icy landscapes, food is scarce, so they must also remember to bring all the food they will need for the trip and extra, in case of emergencies.

A camera is not the only piece of equipment tourists need when visiting Antarctica!

The safest way to travel to the poles is with experienced guides who know how to deal with icebergs and the other ice dangers people face there.

Survival Kit

People also need to make sure they always carry a survival kit. This is a set of useful items that they can use to help survive in an emergency. It should include tools such as a radio, GPS, satellite phone, knife, fishhooks and fishing line, wire, and a shovel or pickax. It could also include water-purifying tablets, equipment to start fires, and an alert beacon or mirror that can send signals.

Emergency items and a well-stocked first aid kit should be carried in a strong, lightweight box or bag made of a waterproof material with a waterproof seal. This will keep them from getting damp or wet, and ensure they can still be used to help people survive in emergencies.

Do or Die

Injuries can weaken you and can prove fatal. To survive at the poles, you will need to have a first aid kit. When on a trip, should you keep your first aid kit in:

a A box at base camp?

b A pocket?

c A strong, lightweight box or bag made of a waterproof material with a waterproof seal?

ANSWERS

Would you survive if you were on your own and stranded on the ice? Check your answers against these correct ones to see if you know how to survive.

Pages 6–7
Answer: B

Layers made from modern, breathable materials are best. Breathable materials allow moisture to escape, so the clothes do not become wet and make the wearer even colder.

Pages 8–9
Answer: A

It is important to wear walking boots that fit correctly to avoid frostbite. Ill-fitting boots may restrict the feet and increase the risk of toe damage.

Pages 10–11
Answer: A

You should never risk your eyes by walking in polar regions without eye protection. Sunlight reflects off snow, so just covering the top of the eyes will not be enough. The sun reflects off the snow and ice up toward the face.

Pages 12–13
Answer: A

Explorers tie tent strings to stone and weigh down their tents with rocks to keep winds from blowing them away.

Pages 14–15
Answer: C

You should make a tunnel cave. You will not be able to build an igloo without a saw or long knife because you need to make even blocks that fit together without gaps, so they prevent wind and cold getting in.

Pages 16–17
Answer: B

Even if you are not hungry, you have to eat enough calories for your body to keep warm in the icy conditions. Take extra food in case of emergencies.

Pages 18–19
Answer: A

A small ice hole is safest for fishing. If you make a bigger hole, there is a greater chance that the ice will crack. Never catch a fish with bare hands, because the water will be freezing and you may get hypothermia.

Pages 20–21
Answer: C

Melting ice in your mouth will make your body temperature drop rapidly. Gray-white Arctic ice is young ice and will contain salt. Melt and drink only blue Arctic ice, because that is older, and the salt has drained out of it.

Pages 22–23

Answer: C

Black ice is dangerous because it is only newly frozen, so it is the weakest type of ice. Gray ice is thicker, but the safest ice is white ice, which is at least 6 to 12 inches (15 to 30 cm) thick.

Pages 24–25

Answer: A

A compass needle always points north. To the left of north on the compass is west. To the right is east, and directly below north is south.

Pages 26–27

Answer: B

To spread your weight over a wider area, you need shoes that are broad and flat, a little like the head of a tennis racket. Just wrapping plastic bags over your shoes will not help, neither will making shoes higher.

Pages 28–29

Answer: B

If you act aggressively, you should be able to scare off the wolf. However, if you turn and run away or look scared, this may make the wolf attack.

Pages 30–31

Answer: B

To escape a polar bear, you need to scare it off or disable it for a moment, to allow you to escape. Pepper spray stings a bear's eyes for a short time, giving you the chance to get to safety. Do not walk toward the bear because it will attack, and lying down will just make you an easier target.

Pages 32–33

Answer: C

The most important advice for avoiding a leopard seal attack is to keep away from the edge of the ice.

Pages 34–35

Answer: A

Use a pole to test the thickness of ice because you can hold it out ahead of you. It is long, so it can give you a better idea of depth. A knife is too short, and it is too cold to put your hand in the ice.

Pages 36–37

Answer: B

People cannot hear you in a blizzard because the winds are so loud. The best action to take is to grab a blizz line, and follow it to safety.

Pages 38–39

Answer: B

The best way to avoid icebergs is to plot a course according to IIP sightings. It is useful to look out for icebergs, too, but remember that 99 percent of an iceberg is under the water.

Pages 40–41

Answer: C

You should travel in teams of about three people roped together, so you will need four ropes.

Pages 42–43

Answer: C

You should keep a first aid kit with you at all times (not back at camp), and it should be in a watertight container to keep items inside from getting damp and becoming useless.

GLOSSARY

adapted suited to an environment or habitat

amputated cut off

antifreeze a substance that keeps car radiators from freezing in winter

blubber the thick layer of fat found under some animals' skin

calories units used to measure the amount of energy in food

camouflages hides by using special features, such as white fur

carbon monoxide a colorless, odorless, tasteless, poisonous gas that can be released when fuel is burned

caterpillar tracks endless metal belt around the wheels of a vehicle that help it move over rough ground

climate the average weather conditions found in an area

climate change changes in weather patterns believed to be caused by human activity, such as burning fuels

contaminated dirty with germs or poisonous

continent one of the seven large landmasses on Earth

dehydrated not having enough water in the body

dome a type of curved roof

evaporates turns from liquid into a gas

filtered passed something, such as water, through a mesh to remove dirt

generators machines that produce or make electricity

glacier a large, very slow-moving mass of ice

global positioning system (GPS) a system that helps people find their location on a map

habitat a place in nature where animals live

hulls the bodies of boats or ships

hypothermia a condition in which the body gets too cold to function

icebreakers large ships designed for breaking a path through ice

ice sheets masses of glacier ice that cover a large area of land

insulating keeping heat or cold from moving from one place to another

navigate to find one's way around

navigation equipment devices used to find one's way around

orbits moves in a path in space around a star or planet

pepper spray a substance made from peppers that temporarily hurts the eyes, nose, throat, and skin when it is sprayed on a person or animal

predators animals that hunt and eat other animals

prey an animal that is hunted and eaten by other animals

radar a device that sends out radio waves to discover the position and speed of a moving object

satellite phone a telephone that works using electronic devices high in space that move around Earth

snow blindness a condition caused by exposure to bright sunlight. It may lead to permanent blindness.

thermals items made of a fabric that provides insulation to keep a person's body warm

tissues the materials that form body parts

ultraviolet (UV) invisible rays given off by the sun that can harm human skin and eyes

FOR MORE INFORMATION

Books

Antarctic Expedition (DK Adventures). New York, NY: DK Publishing, 2015.

Blake, Kevin. *Lost in the Antarctic* (Stranded!: Testing the Limits of Survival). New York, NY: Bearport Publishing, 2014.

Petersen, Christine. *Learning about Antarctica* (Searchlight Books Do You Know the Continents?). Minneapolis, MN: Lerner Classroom, 2015.

Seiple, Samantha. *Byrd & Igloo: A Polar Adventure*. New York, NY: Scholastic, 2013.

Websites

Read about climate change and the Arctic at:
http://climatekids.nasa.gov/arctic-animals

Read the World Wide Fund for nature fact file about the Arctic at:
http://gowild.wwf.org.uk/regions/polar-fact-files/the-arctic

Check out 10 facts about the Arctic at:
www.ngkids.co.uk/places/ten-facts-about-the-arctic

Publisher's note to educators and parents: Our editors have carefully reviewed these websites to ensure that they are suitable for students. Many websites change frequently, however, and we cannot guarantee that a site's future contents will continue to meet our high standards of quality and educational value. Be advised that students should be closely supervised whenever they access the Internet.

INDEX